Kiddiwalks

IN
WEST SUSSEX

Len Markham

COUNTRYSIDE BOOKS
NEWBURY BERKSHIRE

◆◆◆◆◆◆◆◆◆◆◆◆◆◆◆◆◆◆◆◆◆◆◆◆◆◆◆◆◆◆◆◆◆◆◆

First published 2006
© Len Markham, 2006

COUNTRYSIDE BOOKS
3 Catherine Road
Newbury, Berkshire

To view our complete range of books,
please visit us at
www.countrysidebooks.co.uk

ISBN 1 85306 954 X
EAN 978 1 85306 954 3

*For my mother Ethel Elizabeth Markham, who
discovered the tops in the end, and for my father
Leonard Markham who encouraged my first steps.*

Photographs by the author

Designed by Peter Davies, Nautilus Design

Produced through MRM Associates Ltd., Reading
Typeset by Techniset Typesetters, Newton-le-Willows
Printed by Woolnough Bookbinding Ltd., Irthlingborough

Contents

Contents

◆ ◆

PUBLISHER'S NOTE

We hope that you obtain considerable enjoyment from this book; great care has been taken in its preparation. Although at the time of publication all routes followed public rights of way or permitted paths, diversion orders can be made and permissions withdrawn.

We cannot, of course, be held responsible for such diversion orders and any inaccuracies in the text which result from these or any other changes to the routes nor any damage which might result from walkers trespassing on private property. We are anxious though that all details covering the walks are kept up to date and would therefore welcome information from readers which would be relevant to future editions.

The simple sketch maps that accompany the walks in this book are based on notes made by the author whilst checking out the routes on the ground. However, for the benefit of a proper map, we do recommend that you purchase the relevant Ordnance Survey sheet covering your walk. The Ordnance Survey maps are widely available, especially through booksellers and local newsagents.

Introduction

I knew I was on to a winner after the completion of my book *Kiddiwalks in East Sussex* when my young grandson asked me for a pair of walking boots for Christmas. And he's just out of nappies! I really enjoyed my adventures in the eastern half of the county and set out to explore her western sister with great anticipation, wondering what exciting discoveries awaited me. I was not disappointed.

West Sussex is just a little more refined and sophisticated than its twin but the subtle differences are no more than the tinkle of a tea cup, the western half of the county, with its chalk-duveted downs, beautiful manicured towns and villages and lively seaside resorts drawing émigrés from London and seasonal visitors by the thousand.

The county is a landscape-rich one, offering a wealth of walking opportunities for novice pedestrians on gentle tracks. In devising these routes, however, after introducing young legs to the paths in East Sussex, I'm encouraging youngsters to stride out a little and tackle slightly more taxing walks, our excursions taking us up an eminence whose view was described by John Constable as 'the grandest in the world', to the top of a 2,000-year-old hill fort where I enjoyed a profusion of butterflies – I've not seen such a spectacle in over 5,000 miles of walking – and to a downland summit used by a legendary giant as a chair! Mostly though, these walks are on short level routes – 15 of them are under 3 miles in length – that can be accomplished by the youngest of children. Some walks are suitable for toddlers and for buggies.

My long experience of family walking excursions has been a thoroughly enjoyable and happy one. Even before they could walk, my children were 'blooded' on the Yorkshire hills from the wonderful vantage point of a papoose. I cannot recommend this Red Indian inspired contraption highly enough. As a parent – apart from the time my passenger masticated a nectarine and dripped juice all down my back – I loved taking baby to see the heights. It's amazing what they see and appreciate from the comfort of dad's back. And, when they're old enough, take them down and let them stretch their legs, encouraging them to pant to the top and push

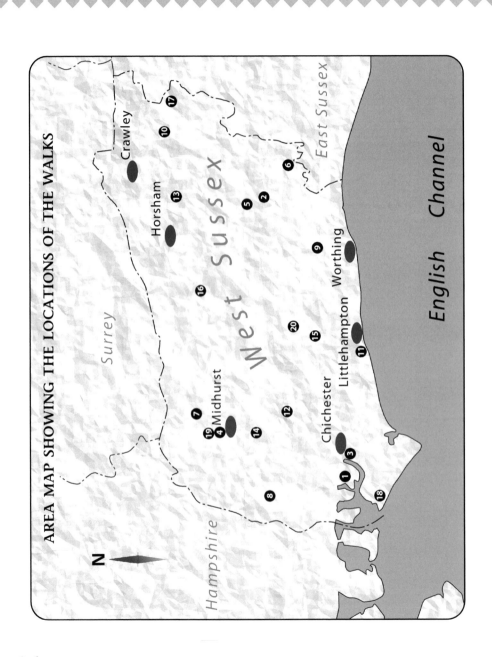

AREA MAP SHOWING THE LOCATIONS OF THE WALKS

◆◆◆◆◆◆◆◆◆◆◆◆◆◆◆◆◆◆◆◆◆◆◆◆◆◆◆◆◆◆◆

their little Union Jacks in the turf. You'll make walkers of them yet and they'll remember their blessed days in the Sussex countryside all their lives.

In these pages, you'll find a great variety of walks that take you into all types of attractive places, villages and wildlife habitats. You'll visit the spectacular Arundel to wander around its castle and through its regal park, you'll creep wide-eyed through a forest noted for its terrible dragon, you'll wander around Chichester Marina and see some of the most expensive vessels afloat, you'll follow quiet rivers and canals alive with flowers and birds and haul up on a beach fronting a spectacular river estuary with long distance views of the Isle of Wight.

Each walk in the book is presented in as user friendly a manner as possible. Routes are briefly described and key information is given about locations, starting points, parking, mileages, time durations of walks and refreshment opportunities. There is also a section headed 'Fun Things to See and Do' giving details of such attractions as museums and steam railways and opportunities for windsurfing, bike hire, boating and fishing. I've also appended background walk-relevant notes to enhance the enjoyment of the walks.

The sketch maps that accompany each walk are meant as general route guides but I do also recommend that parents invest in the quoted OS maps. These identify other fascinating features in the Sussex countryside, and add to the enjoyment of the walks.

In my own small way, I have a mission to re-introduce young people to the delights of using their own legs and enjoying the marvels of the English countryside. I hope this book and its companion volume *Kiddiwalks in East Sussex*, helps local children to discover their own county, a county described 75 years ago by a fellow tramp as ' ... the real Sussex, the country that stands on the chalk, the high downland with its flocks, its close-cropped grass, its windy peaks, giving distant views of the sea, and above all that open, pastoral atmosphere that can turn the most self-conscious slave of the conventions of towns into the happiest and most careless vagabond'.

Len Markham

1

Bosham

Up a Creek With a Paddle

Quay Meadow, Bosham.

A sleepy old and unspoilt fishing community whose rhythms run with the tides, Bosham was once famous for its oysters and boat building. Overlooking a quiet creek with its own channel to the sea, the village is clustered around the Mill Stream, the sea paying regular courtesy calls, at high tide, to cottages with nautical names like the Old Ship, The Galleon, Before Anchor and Mariners Cottage. A relaxing place where only the gulls and the sounds of flapping sails break the silence, Bosham has a unique National Trust meadow near its quay, a venerable church which is the oldest site of Christianity in Sussex and a rambling main street where you are likely to encounter more boats than cars.

This gentle amble follows Waterfront Road to the quay and the meadow, visiting High Street and an expanse of mudflats before returning on a raised causeway back into the village.

Bosham

◆ ◆

 Getting there *Bosham is about 3 miles west of Chichester. Leave the A259 roundabout at Broad Bridge and go south on the minor road for 1 mile, following the signs.*

Length of walk 1/2 mile.
Time 1 hour.
Terrain Flat lanes and footpaths with a few steps at the end. Children will enjoy poking in the mudflats and wellies might be the appropriate footwear. The walk is suitable for buggies and pushchairs if help is on hand with the steps.
Start/Parking Park in the pay-and-display car park (toilets available on site) signposted left off Bosham Lane as you approach Waterfront Road (GR 806040).
Map OS Explorer 120 Chichester, South Harting & Selsey.
Refreshments The Anchor Bleu inn on High Street serves good quality bar food with daily specials. It has an inviting rear patio garden. Telephone: 01243 573956.

The Walk

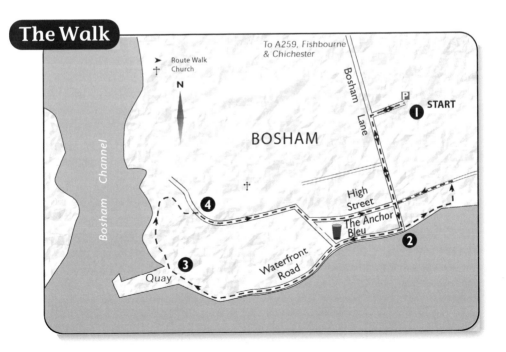

9 ◆

Kiddiwalks in West Sussex

◆◆*1*◆◆◆◆◆◆◆◆◆◆◆◆◆◆◆◆◆◆◆◆◆◆◆◆◆◆◆◆

❶ From the car park, follow the sign to the harbour and the village and turn left on Bosham Lane.

❷ Turn right at the water's edge (it is prone to flooding at high tide) on Waterfront Road and proceed past the Anchor Bleu inn and the Water Mill to the Quay.

❸ Swing right over the National Trust's Quay Meadow and swing right again past the war memorial on the lane to the National Trust sign.

❹ Go left on a bridge over the Mill Stream and proceed down High Street, passing the back of the Anchor Bleu inn. Walk on to the junction with Bosham Lane.

◆ Fun Things to See and Do ◆

Feeding the swans and ducks and fishing with nets on the mudflats.

And can children find the Crusaders' Crosses on the doorway of the inner porch of **Holy Trinity church**? These were made by crusaders returning from the Holy Land. As a dedication to thanksgiving and peace, they blunted their weapons on the stone by inscribing a cross.

Bosham Walk Art and Craft Centre (almost opposite the pedestrian route to the car park). Its old world setting houses 19 artists and craftsmen's shops on two floors. Children are encouraged to try out new skills such as painting and jewellery making. Telephone: 01243 572475.

Fishbourne Roman Palace is $1^1/_2$ miles east of Bosham (signposted off the A259). Regarded as the finest Roman residence in Britain, its treasures include fantastic mosaics, a bath suite, corridors and a period garden established on the original plan. Seasonal events include half-term family fun days, and a Roman Army Week when children can become a legionary for a day. Telephone: 01243 785859.

◆◆◆◆◆◆◆◆◆◆◆◆◆◆◆◆◆◆◆◆◆◆◆◆◆◆◆◆

5 Go right and immediately left on Waterfront Road and pass the little tower, continuing for about 350 yards. Go left up the steps onto the raised causeway and go left again, weaving right back to Bosham Lane. Turn right on the outward route back to the car park.

The quay side at Bosham is full of interest.

◆ Background Notes ◆

Tradition suggests that in much earlier times **Bosham** – pronounced Bozzam – was a favourite haunt of the Roman Emperor Vespasian and the last resting place of a daughter of King Canute. There's even a legend that the old king got his feet and his throne wet at Bosham. You'll be in good company!

Part of Bosham's Saxon church is depicted in the **Bayeux Tapestry**, one panel showing King Harold kneeling to pray in the church before his unsuccessful journey to Normandy in 1064.

The **marvellous giant Bevis**, who is also encountered on the walks in Arundel and Compton, would often pause in Bosham to wash his dogs. He would linger in the village and drink a barrel or two on his way from Southampton to Arundel. He possessed a telephone-pole-sized staff, which he used when wading from the Isle of Wight, and bequeathed it at his death to Bosham church where it was used for many years as a flagpole.

Woods Mill, Henfield

Nature Trail

Little dippers.

Woods Mill, Henfield

◆◆◆◆◆◆◆◆◆◆◆◆◆◆◆◆◆◆◆◆◆◆◆◆◆◆◆◆◆◆◆◆◆◆◆◆◆◆◆

Centred around an old flour mill and its defunct but elaborate water supply system, Woods Mill must be one of the most successful and easily accessible nature reserves in the country. With great vision, the derelict site was acquired by the county's leading wildlife charity, the Sussex Wildlife Trust having created a wonderful wildlife showcase that is especially suitable for young children. The reserve allows youngsters – particularly those in organised parties – to get close up and intimate with plants, flowers, insects, invertebrates and birds. Leaflets and a welter of spotter information, activity sheets, signposted trails, information boards, viewing areas, field kits and fishing nets and a bird hide all serve to heighten the experience. And will you discover the mysterious stones hidden in the wood? Entry and car parking are free.

 Getting there *Woods Mill is on the A2037 between Henfield and Castle Town north of Shoreham-on-Sea. Look out for the direction sign to Woodmancote.*

Length of walk 1 mile.
Time 1 hour.
Terrain Levelled gravel paths suitable for children of all ages and for pushchairs and buggies.

Start/Parking Park in the designated car park (GR 217137) off Horn Lane near its junction with the A2037. Toilet facilities are available close by.
Map OS Explorer 122 Brighton & Hove.
Refreshments There are no refreshment facilities on site but the reserve is ideal for spring and summer picnics.

◆ Fun Things to See and Do ◆

 Woods Mill staff will organise **nature visits** for parties of young children.
Telephone: 01273 492630.

Kiddiwalks in West Sussex

The Walk

❶ Take the footpath at the bottom of the car park, crossing the wide bridge over the former mill dam. Go left at the signboard, following the 'Nature Trail' sign. Continue forward with the path and pass the reed bed, swinging right. Go left for a short distance to a gated entrance into the Little Meadow. Go through and make a circuit of the meadow, rejoining the main path. Go left to the top of the lake and a bench.

❷ Swing right and walk lakeside. Go right for a short distance over the bridge to the observation platform overlooking the lake. Return to the main path. Go right and continue to the bottom of the lake.

❸ Go right. Go left for a short distance to the bird hide. Turn left and swing round through coppiced woodland to a pond, crossing two bridges, to regain the main path. Swing left back to the starting point.

Woods Mill, Henfield

◆◆◆◆◆◆◆◆◆◆◆◆◆◆◆◆◆◆◆◆◆◆◆◆◆◆◆◆◆◆◆◆◆

◆ Background Notes ◆

Spring is definitely the best time to visit **Woods Mill**. Every spring season, a number of migratory birds including blackcap, chiff chaff, cuckoo, nightingale, reed warbler, sedge warbler and whitethroat descend on the reserve to breed. You may also see more common species such as tree creeper, nuthatch, tit and kingfisher. Twenty-eight species of butterfly have been recorded at Woods Mill – about 40% of the total found in Britain. A large number of these rely on the leaves and flowers of stinging nettles as part of their life cycles and nettles are allowed to flourish all over the reserve! Butterfly types include brimstone, comma, gatekeeper, meadow brown, painted lady and speckled wood. And look carefully ... there are some enormous fish in the pond!

Sussex Wildlife Trust cares for 36 nature reserves across Sussex and organises a programme of environmental education and family events. Wildlife Watch is the junior branch of the trust. To participate in local events, receive free magazines and get more deeply involved with protecting local wildlife, telephone 01273 492630 and find out how to join.

On a tributary of the River Adur, **the mill** was mentioned as early as 1538. Steam power was installed in 1911. In the 1930s, the mill was used as a tearoom. Milling ceased in 1927 and the property was left to deteriorate until it was bequeathed to the trust in 1966.

3

Chichester Marina

Before the Masts

This marina is one of the largest in the UK.

his is what becomes of messing about with boats in the bath. Ellen MacArthur had a toy yacht as a child and look where that led! Chichester has one of the biggest marinas in the country, over eleven hundred beautiful craft crowding into a most imaginatively converted former saltworks. Here, the chic, sophisticated and very expensive exists cheek by prow with wild nature, pastoral scenes of cows grazing just a few strides from the berths and distant calls of one of the most secretive birds in the world booming from nearby reed beds, harmoniously blending with the razzmatazz sights and sounds of making ready for sea.

This short but eye-popping walk – 'Can we have one of those, Dad?' – circuits the marina, stopping off at a bird hide. Here you may discover reed buntings, reed warblers, bearded reedlings, little egrets, ospreys, sparrowhawks, black tailed godwits, kingfishers, avocets and the most secretive bird of them all – the bittern. Our route passes over a lock-top walkway where you will linger and enjoy the to-and-fro cavalcade of boats. Part of the path then follows the route of the water-lily-carpeted Chichester Canal, now occupied by a collection of quaint houseboats ... each one with its own letterbox!

◆◆◆◆◆◆◆◆◆◆◆◆◆◆◆◆◆◆◆◆◆◆◆◆◆◆◆◆◆◆◆◆

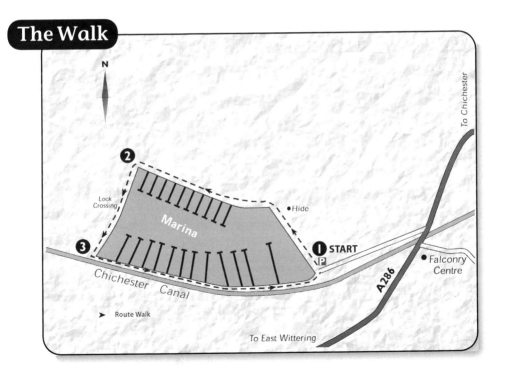

Getting there *Chichester Marina is around 3 miles south of the town. Leave the A27 bypass on the A286 and turn second right just before Cutfield Bridge, following the prominent sign up the access road (road humps) to the car park.*

Length of walk 1 mile.
Time 1 hour.
Terrain Level concrete/asphalt footpaths all the way. Suitable for buggies and pushchairs.
Start/Parking Park in the marina's free car park (GR 836011).
Map OS Explorer 120 Chichester, South Harting & Selsey.
Refreshments The Spinnaker Café and Restaurant (on the route of the walk) offers light snacks and more substantial meals such as steak and fresh fish. Telephone: 01243 511032.

The Walk

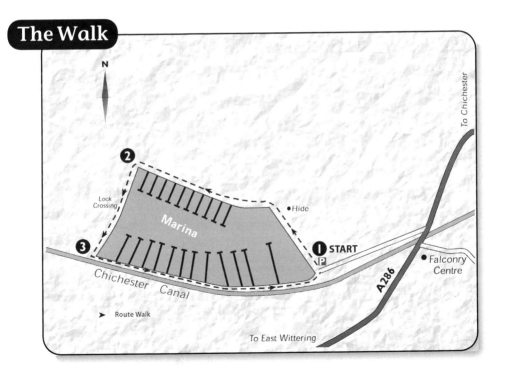

Kiddiwalks in West Sussex

3

① Turn right from the car park and follow the sign to the bird hide. Visit the hide and continue to the marina corner.

② Go left and cross the lock gate footway. Pass Peter's Shipyard to reach the next corner.

③ Turn left, following the public footpath sign, and pass the Spinnaker Café and Restaurant. Walk on and turn left back to the car park.

◆ Fun Things to See and Do ◆

Bring binoculars and a field guide to enable children to get the most from their visit to the **marina bird hide**.

The nearby **Sussex Falconry Centre** in Waphams Lane, Birdham, directly opposite Chichester Marina, exhibits birds of prey such as falcons, hawks, eagles, owls and vultures. The birds are flown daily in spectacular displays of flight and hunting techniques. The centre, which is open Tuesday to Sunday, runs full day courses for children and adults. Telephone: 01243 512472.

Now you've seen the luxury yachts, join them on the ocean waves by taking a leisurely voyage of your own, **Chichester Harbour Water Tours** organising daily sailings with full commentaries about the port and its history. There are four excursions a day in summer. Check sailing time by ringing the talking timetable on 01243 670504.

The **Mechanical Music and Doll Collection** in Church Road, Portfield, Chichester has a fascinating collection of over 100 Victorian and Edwardian dolls that will engage children, other exhibits including restored musical boxes, barrel-organs and fairground organs. Open Wednesdays only from June to September. Telephone: 01243 372646,

Boats waiting to leave the lock chamber at Chichester Marina.

◆ Background Notes ◆

Chichester Marina was excavated from the marshy remains of a former saltworks. The development successfully incorporates three distinct habitats, reed beds, wetland and an inter-tidal zone and salt marshes. The former Appledram Saltworks was constructed in the 18th century. Seawater was collected in shallow, clay lined pools and left to evaporate. The resultant briny liquor was boiled to drive off the remaining moisture, producing high quality salt crystals used in medicine and in the preservation of meat and fish. The industry began to decline in the early 1820s as a consequence of the high cost of fuel and crippling taxes and it was eventually closed and the site abandoned.

The **Chichester Canal** was part of the Portsmouth and Arundel Canal, which linked with London. Opened in 1822, it was operated until 1855 but is now used for a variety of leisure activities including fishing, canoeing and boating.

4

Midhurst

Polo Exploration

This building stands on staddle stones.

M idhurst is one of the most attractive market towns in the whole of West Sussex. With its web of old streets lined higgledy piggledy with timber framed cottages on Duck Street, Wool Street, June Lane and Knockhundred Row, it cries out for a closer look, the nearby banks of a delightful river and the precincts of a derelict castle and internationally famous polo fields adding to a charm that brings visitors by the thousand.

This short but interesting amble begins by treading the hallowed polo fields and circuiting the ruins of Cowdray Castle, our path following the looping banks of the River Rother back into the town along several of its ancient thoroughfares.

◆◆◆◆◆◆◆◆◆◆◆◆◆◆◆◆◆◆◆◆◆◆◆◆◆◆◆◆◆◆◆

 Getting there *Midhurst is at the junction of the A272 and the A286 around 10 miles north of Chichester.*

Length of walk 1¹/₂ miles.
Time 2 hours.
Terrain Flat pavements, field tracks and paths with one short, stepped ascent.
Start/Parking Park in one of the town's pay-and-display car parks. The car park adjacent to the start of this walk at the Tourist Information Centre on North Street (GR 886217) is the most convenient and it has toilet facilities.
Map OS Explorer 133 Haslemere & Petersfield.
Refreshments There is a wonderful choice of refreshment options in Midhurst, numerous period pubs, chic bistros and restaurants and a host of cafés competing for business.

◆ Fun Things to See and Do ◆

 The local Cowdray Estate is famed as the home of British **polo**. International matches are staged during the season between April and October. Children under 12 have free entry. Telephone: 01730 812423.

Petworth Park, around 7 miles east of Midhurst on the A272, is a magnificent National Trust mansion set in a 700 acre deer park. Children will particularly enjoy its extensive servants' quarters, the 'below stairs' tour and quizzes. Telephone: 01798 342207.

The Walk

To Petworth

N

A272

Tourist
Information
Centre

Polo
Grounds

START

● Tower

To Trotton

MIDHURST ❸

❷

Cowdray
ruins

❹

A272

❺

A286

River Rother

To Cocking

➤ Route Walk
✝ Church

❶ Start at the Tourist Information Centre at the north end of North Road. Show the children the old horse trough marked with the legend 'Drink and Pray' and the modern sundial on the façade of the TIC. Turn right, following the sign to 'Cowdray Ruins'. Go through a gate and walk towards the derelict castle and cross the bridge over the River Rother.

❷ Go left along the lane for 250 yards. Turn right through a gate and walk on the concreted path to the right of the residence known as the Tower. Swing right towards the rugby field and continue over the grass between the ruins and the rugby posts. Swing right by the cottages and go left and right past the intriguing little building on mushroom stilts. Turn right back to the bridge and cross.

❸ Turn left and follow the riverbank down to the bend.

The ruins of Cowdray Castle.

Kiddiwalks in West Sussex

◆◆*4*◆◆◆◆◆◆◆◆◆◆◆◆◆◆◆◆◆◆◆◆◆◆◆◆◆◆◆

4 Swing right through a kissing gate and walk on to the next bend. Keep forward, going uphill and left up the steps. Swing right by the bench and follow the hedge down to a gate. Go through onto St Anne's Hill and swing right to the church and the Swan Inn on Market Square.

5 Turn right to pass the war memorial and proceed on Church Hill, swinging left on Knockhundred Row and turning right on Chichester Road back to the start.

◆ Background Notes ◆

Cowdray Park was built in the reign of Henry VIII. Queen Elizabeth I visited the mansion in August 1591, her party consuming three oxen and 140 geese for breakfast! The estate was owned by the Viscounts Montague, an ancestor of whom evicted the monks from their monastery at Battle Abbey. Outraged, one of the brethren put a curse on the family, predicting that the line would be violently ended by fire and water. Cowdray Park was destroyed by fire in 1793 and the last Viscount Montague was subsequently drowned in the River Rhine. The ruins have a resident ghost – The White Lady of Cowdray.

The local **grammar school** was founded in 1672. The famous author H.G. Wells was a student-teacher there.

In the 17th century, the town was a **centre for weaving** specialising in coarse quilts.

5

Shermanbury

Up a Lazy River

A tranquil scene on the River Adur.

This short and languid walk from Mock Bridge plays peek-a-boo with the infant River Adur, a rather bashful and indolent child that flows gently between reed fringed banks. Swans glide in the pools between rafts of water lilies, herons stand sentinel in the shallows and all about, in summer, are the flutters of butterflies and the drones of a myriad insects. Our route passes the mansion of Shermanbury Place and the tiny ancient church of St Giles, the path skirting a lake by the intriguingly named Shiprods Farm before returning to the bridge over water meadows.

Kiddiwalks in West Sussex

5

Getting there
*Shermanbury is 2 miles
north of Henfield on the
A281.*

Length of walk 1³/₄ miles.
Time 2 hours.
Terrain Field and bankside
paths, some luxuriant and
overgrown in places – long
trousers are recommended.
Start/Parking The walk starts
immediately opposite the Bull
Inn, which has a car park for
customers. Please seek permission
from the staff before leaving your
car (GR 212182). Otherwise, you
could leave your car in the picnic

area 300 yards to the south. I
would recommend, however, that
you use the pub car park as the
A281 is a fast road and there is
no footway.
Map OS Explorer 122 Brighton &
Hove.
Refreshments The Bull Inn. This
inviting roadside inn near Mock
Bridge serves speciality pizzas,
something called Adur tuna (the
fish run big in these parts!) and a
separate children's menu. There
is a modern generously equipped
children's play area adjacent to
an attractive beer garden and an
indoor skittles alley. Telephone:
01273 492232.

◆ Fun Things to See and Do ◆

Why not hire the alley at the Bull Inn and organise a
skittles tournament?

Around 10 miles south of Shermanbury down the
A281, the A2037 and
the A283 is **Old Shoreham Aiport**.
Pleasure flights take off
from here. Telephone:
01344 874515.

Shermanbury

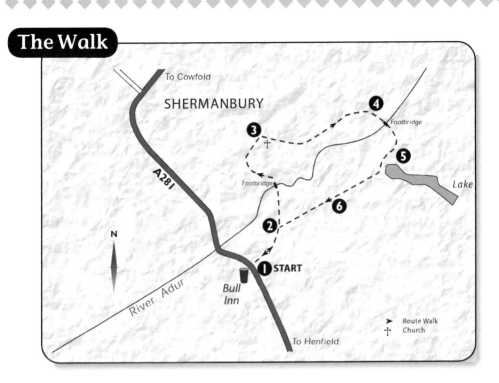

The Walk

❶ Cross the road from the Bull Inn and follow the footpath sign through the hedge right. Go over a planked bridge across a ditch and walk left towards the river. Steer right to a stile. Cross and swing right over a planked bridge between two large trees and walk on to a three-point marker post.

❷ Walk over the water meadow to a signpost and a footbridge. Cross the river and walk on, swinging right through a rusted gate into a small wood and then going left to the signposts.

❸ Turn right on a wide track, passing Shermanbury Place and St Giles' church. Walk on to the three-point sign.

❹ Turn right to the footbridge by the pumping station and re-cross the river, keeping straight forward on an overgrown path.

❺ Turn right, following a public footpath sign along a fence line. Cross a stile and follow the direction arrow right, passing a lake. Cross a second stile and a planked footbridge and go over a

27

third stile, keeping forward and swinging right to a point opposite the house with the big chimneys.

❻ Turn right, following the footpath sign alongside a bramble hedge down to a gate for 20 yards. (Caution: it is easy to take the wrong footpath here and follow the broad turfy path that begins just beyond the gatepost to the right.) Go through the gate and swing left, continuing over the water meadow to the outward three-point sign. Follow the outward route back to the inn.

View from the River Adur.

◆ Background Notes ◆

The **Adur** is a small, gently flowing, heavily reeded river that travels south for about 10 miles to its estuary at Shoreham-on-Sea. It was once harnessed to drive the wheels of local mills, Shermanbury's mill dating from the time of Domesday. The last mill was erected here in 1816.

During the Second World War, large contingents of troops were camped in **Shermanbury Park**.

6

Poynings

The Grandest View in the World

The view from Devil's Dyke.

The South Downs inland from Brighton swirl up to the sky like petrified waves, the levelled crests affording some of the finest views in England. The unassailable tops were coveted by ancient man, entrenchments, the sites of Iron Age forts and scores of tumuli attesting to the strategic and religious significant of places that still excite awe and wonder. And one such top is more wondrous than all the rest, Devil's Dyke, commanding views that sweep half the county and beyond, the famous painter John Constable – and he knew about landscapes! – describing the panorama as 'the grandest in the world'.

This walk from Poynings – a pretty village that took root at the foot of the downs over a thousand years ago – is breathtaking in every sense, the precipitous path leading up through National Trust woodland taking you onto hillsides smothered in wild flowers during the spring and summer months. For your added delight and information, at the summit are three illustrated topography boards that identify the horizon scene, distant landmarks including the highest hill in Kent, Ashdown Forest and the Isle of Wight, some 46 miles to the south-west. There is also a talking telescope!

Kiddiwalks in West Sussex

◆◆6◆◆◆◆◆◆◆◆◆◆◆◆◆◆◆◆◆◆◆◆◆◆◆◆◆◆◆

 Getting there *Poynings is easily accessed off the A23 – the Brighton to London road. Some 3 miles north of the A23/ A27 junction, turn westwards on the A281 and continue for just over 1 mile, keeping straight forward at the bend and following the signposted road to the village.*

Length of walk 1³/₄ miles.
Time 2 hours.
Terrain Undulating grit and turf paths with one short but very steep ascent up a stepped incline (not recommended for children under seven years old).

Start/Parking Park in the Royal Oak car park (GR 263120), if you intend to use the pub (please ask permission from the landlord), or on the road close by.
Map OS Landranger 122 Brighton & Hove.
Refreshments The upmarket Royal Oak serves a sophisticated bistro-type menu with daily specials such as confit of duck. It has a delightful beer garden. Telephone: 01273 857389. At the summit of the hill is the Devil's Dyke pub offering a standard range of food including children's portions of roast beef and Yorkshire pudding. Telephone: 01273 857256.

◆ Fun Things to See and Do ◆

Wild flowers grow in abundance on Devil's Dyke – as many as forty different species per square yard blossom on the grassy slopes in season – and young children will enjoy discovering their names and habits, assisted by a good field book.

A frequent **open top daily bus service to Brighton Pier** operates from a stop outside the Devil's Dyke pub in summer. Two children go free when travelling with an adult. Telephone: 01273 886200. This walk can be combined with a trip to Brighton, its multiple attractions including its pier, beach and extraordinary Royal Pavilion (telephone: 01273 290900).

The Walk

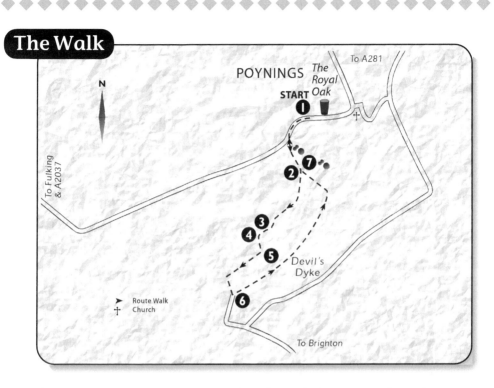

1 Turn right from the Royal Oak for 40 yards and go left down Dyke Lane. Walk on the path to the base of the hill and the National Trust sign.

2 Turn right, following the footpath sign, and weave left up the steps, following the yellow arrow marker through woodland.

3 Go right through a kissing gate and continue climbing up the steps on a track heading towards the top of a valley to your left.

4 Go left up a rough track, climbing steeply to a stile.

5 Cross right and walk on to a white marker post, going left to towards the telescope and the topography boards. Go to the right of the Devil's Dyke pub, passing the Brighton Pier bus stop, and continue to a point just beyond the pub car park.

6 Go left, following the arrow markers, and walk along a path above the valley to the right. Merge with a track and continue

The old service bus to Devil's Dyke, now in the Amberley Working Museum (see Walk 20).

◆◆◆◆◆◆◆◆◆◆◆◆◆◆◆◆◆◆◆◆◆◆◆◆◆◆◆◆◆◆◆

to a gate. Go through and descend, swinging left into woodland, and go through a gate. Keep dropping down to the outward National Trust sign.

❼ Turn right along the outward route back to the start.

◆ Background Notes ◆

Legend has it that the Devil was so disgusted at the proliferation of churches in Sussex that he resolved to destroy the entire county by drowning, seeking to dig a channel to the sea overnight and cause a massive flood. He began his excavations at Poynings and dug with such fury that he created Cissbury Ring (see Walk 9), Chanctonbury Ring, Rackham Hill and Mount Caburn. The tremendous din of his digging disturbed an old Poynings woman from her slumbers and she resolved, with God's help, to save the county. She lit a candle and magnified its light in a glass jar, simulating sunrise. Simultaneously, she prodded her sleeping cockerel and had him crow, the combined ruse persuading the Devil that dawn had come. With mighty petulance, he abandoned his task half finished and flew away, a large clod from his hoof dropping to create the Isle of Wight!

In our grandparents' time, **the Devil's Dyke was a real tourist attraction.** A railway ran to Poynings from Brighton until the 1930s and a funicular railway connected the village with the summit up to the turn of the last century.

7

Henley

You're Sure of a Big Surprise

Feeding the fish.

C oaches and six once approached the brow of the cliff overlooking
Henley and the horses shivered with fright at the prospect of the
descent, this ancient staging post on the main highway between
London and Chichester breaking more wheels than Maximus in
Gladiator. Henley owes its existence to its strategic position and its
ancient inn but the through traffic and the snorting horses have long
gone, a 19th century bypass leaving the hamlet and its delightful Duke
of Cumberland Arms for the surprising discovery of fortunate visitors.

As invigorating as it is – a feast for the senses with sighing trees,
aromatic smells of beech and pine and cool forest shade all the way in
summer – this walk has competition from the inn, its wooded 3^1/$_2$ acres
alpine-like garden set with three trout-filled ponds also inviting
exploration. But drink up and off we go!

Getting there *Henley is 2¹/₂ miles north of Midhurst just off the A286. The access from the top of the hill is still a little tricky and the approach from the hill bottom, off the bypass, is recommended.*

Distance 2 miles.
Time 2 hours.
Terrain Steadily ascending/descending shaded woodland tracks throughout, which can be muddy in places after heavy rain. The walk is cool and pleasant in hot weather and is best reserved for summer days.

Start/Parking Park in the Duke of Cumberland Arms car park, asking permission from the staff first (GR 895257) or alongside the lane.
Map OS Explorer 133 Haslemere & Petersfield.
Refreshments The Duke of Cumberland Arms, an attractive 15th century inn, is picturesquely perched on a hillside, its garden, which incorporates a series of inter-connected, spring-fed trout ponds, providing fine country views and a perfect al fresco dining area for the summer months. Children cannot resist

◆ Fun Things to See and Do ◆

The local Cowdray Estate is famed as the home of British **polo**. International matches are staged during the season between April and October. Children under 12 have free entry. Telephone: 01730 812423.

Petworth Park, around 7 miles east of Midhurst on the A272, is a magnificent National Trust mansion set in a 700 acre deer park. Children will particularly enjoy its extensive servants' quarters, the 'below stairs' tour and quizzes. Telephone: 01798 342207.

Kiddiwalks in West Sussex

◆ ◆ **7** ◆

tossing lunch morsels to the fish – but after their frolics in the garden, the little ones may be too tired for their walk! The menu includes Dover sole and ham and eggs. Telephone: 01428 652280.

The Walk

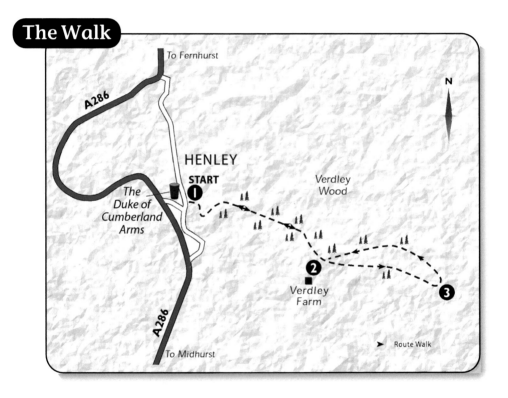

❶ Take the signed footpath immediately opposite the pub by the telephone box. Go left at the bi-directional sign and swing left at the next sign. Swing right over the bridge and keep forward on the broad track. Go straight ahead at the next sign.

❷ Where the track splits three ways, take the higher track right and go uphill, gradually walking up towards the woodland fringe with views right of Verdley Farm. Keep forward to the lane.

❸ Turn round and take the right hand path downhill to rejoin the outward route near the Verdley Farm viewpoint. Return downhill to the start.

◆ Background Notes ◆

The hamlet of **Henley** is delightfully situated in the cradling arms of a hillside with long distance views to the north. It owes its existence to its strategic position on a vital highway, its densely wooded hillsides providing ideal concealment for robbers who operated in the area. Several were apprehended and hanged for their crimes and, as a deterrent, their bodies were left to rot at local crossroads.

The wonderful garden at the Duke of Cumberland Arms.

8

Compton

March Them Up to the Top of the Hill

The sleepy village of Compton.

S nug under the skirts of Telegraph Hill, the little rural hamlet of Compton is less than 5 miles as the crow flies from a busy motorway but it's light years away from the bustle of modern life. As you drive into the village you get the urge to turn off your engine and glide the last few yards, lest you wake up the residents! Surrounded by fields of wheat and sweetcorn in the summer months on hills that race up to the sky, the village with its old church, single store and inviting roadside inn is a perfect base for rambling, our gentle amble taking us through a delectable wood and by way of a millennia-old burial barrow to one of the best viewpoints in the county.

Children will enjoy picking up the trail of the rascal giant Bevis, who we also encounter on the walks at Arundel and Bosham.

Compton

 Getting there *Compton is north-west of Chichester. Approaching from the town, take the B2178 and the B2146 north-west for 6 miles to the junction with the B2147, then, staying on the B2146, go north for 4 1/2 miles.*

Length of walk 2 1/4 miles.
Time 2 hours.
Terrain Field paths and woodland and farm tracks with two gentle ascents/descents.

Start/Parking Park opposite the Coach and Horses in The Square (GR 777147).
Map OS Explorer 120 Chichester, South Harting & Selsey.
Refreshments The Coach and Horses features a medley of meat dishes such as rack of lamb and rib-eye steaks. Telephone: 02392 631228. Uppark (see 'Fun Things to See and Do') has a restaurant serving snacks and daily specials. Telephone: 01730 825415.

The Walk

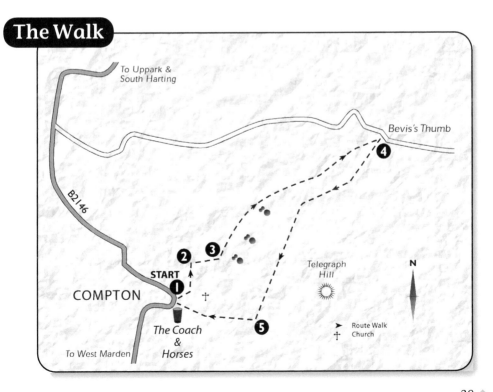

Kiddiwalks in West Sussex

8

1 Walk away from The Square and go left after 100 yards, following a public footpath sign. Swing right through a gate to a concreted stockyard and go left to a stile.

2 Cross and go right uphill on a footpath in the middle of a field.

3 Leave the field and go left along a woodland fringe track at the three-way sign. Leave the wood and keep straight forward to the three-way sign near Bevis's Thumb Long Barrow. *Have a seat here!*

4 Turn right on a track, following the sign, and walk steadily uphill in the direction of the blue arrow marker to the summit of Telegraph Hill. *The imposing residence on the skyline to the north-west is the National Trust property of Uppark.* Continue to the four-directional sign.

5 Turn right and follow the wood edge. Drop down to cross a stile, then walk downhill as indicated by a yellow arrow marker. Fifty yards before the bottom, swing right into the edge of a wood and cross a stile. Follow a yellow arrow marker left on a track, swinging right to a four-directional sign. Keep going right, back to The Square.

◆ Fun Things to See and Do ◆

Immediately north of Compton, 2 miles along the B2146, is the fascinating National Trust property known as **Uppark**. Its atmospheric Victorian servants' rooms and 'below stairs' tunnels, famous dolls' house, games area and quizzes will appeal to children.
Telephone: 01730 825415.

The view from the top of Telegraph Hill.

◆ Background Notes ◆

On **Telegraph Hill** (it was so called after it was used as a semaphore station for relaying messages from Portsmouth Dockyard to the Admiralty in London) is a prehistoric long barrow known as **Bevis's Thumb**. This is in reference to the gentleman giant (see Walks 1 and 15) who was said to have used the mound as a chair! Spithead and the Isle of Wight can be seen from the 534 feet high hill summit.

Uppark was built around 1690. For a time, the mother of H.G. Wells was its housekeeper and the author spent some time living here. The mansion was offered to Wellington after the Napoleonic wars. He is said to have declined the gift suggesting that the surrounding slopes were too steep for his horses! The house was gutted by fire in 1989 but was restored and reopened to the public in 1997.

9

Cissbury

Lords of the Ring

Common centaury flowers on Cissbury Ring.

Whatever your age, Cissbury Ring just has to be climbed, the spirits of our ancestors, who made their citadel homes here 300 years before Christ, drawing you up to gaze and wonder. Surveying half the county and beyond, this special place was a hill fort, its precipitous slopes strengthened by ditches, ramparts and timber palisades, protecting a regional capital of an Iron Age community. One of the best examples of its type in Britain, this prestigious site was the realm of an elite tribe. Miraculously, it has survived largely undisturbed for over 2,000 years.

This short walk through grassland graced in season by rare flowers and myriads of butterflies – in 5,000 miles of walking I've never enjoyed such a profusion – takes you to the top of the Ring at 600 feet above sea level, the return route following the curving line of the old rampart. Bring a butterfly field guide ... and the children's plastic swords!

Getting there *Cissbury Ring is just 2 miles north of Worthing, immediately east of the A24.*

Length of walk 2¼ miles.
Time 2 hours.
Terrain Field paths with two gentle ascents/descents.
Start/Parking Park in the designated free car park (GR 128077). Turn eastwards off the A24 on May Tree Avenue and go first left for a short distance on Storrington Rise.
Map OS Explorer 121 Arundel & Pulborough.
Refreshments The Black Horse at Findon (turn right from May Tree Avenue and go north on the A24 for under a mile). Good bar snacks. Telephone: 01903 872301.

The Walk

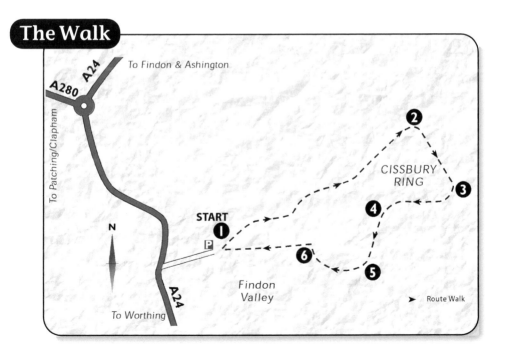

Kiddiwalks in West Sussex

9

❶ From the car park, go left, following the sign 'Cissbury Ring 10 Minutes', swinging right to a gate and going forward. Snake left at the bottom of the rampart and continue to a gate, going through and keeping forward uphill to the lane end and an information board.

❷ Turn right, following the sign, and just before the kissing gate go left uphill on a track. Walk on to the gate.

❸ Go through and turn right, walking through a gate and the breach in the rampart, and continue to the triangulation pillar.

❹ Go left and keep forward, merging with a track from the left. Keep on to the rampart breach.

❺ Go right up the steps onto the rampart and swing right. *From here you can see High Salvington windmill one mile to the south-west.*

❻ Go left down the next flight of steps, dropping off the rampart and passing through two gates. Swing right in the field corner to the bench and go left across the field back to the car park.

◆ Fun Things to See and Do ◆

High Salvington Windmill (it is visible south-west from the rampart) is in working order and is still grinding flour after 250 years. Of the black post type, it originally dates from before 1750. The mill has a restored granary, and a shop and refreshments are available. It is open in the afternoons on the first and third Sundays of each month between April and September. Go right from May Tree Avenue and first left. Telephone: 01903 266628 or 267293.

Just 2 miles south, **Worthing** has an extensive beach and all the attractions of a modern seaside resort.

Cissbury

◆◆◆

◆ Background Notes ◆

Cissbury Ring is one of Britain's greatest prehistoric hill forts. The remains of a vast defensive rampart are over a mile long. It bristled with an imposing palisade of rammed tree trunks – enclosing an area of 65 acres. The summit has magnificent views encompassing the whole of Worthing, the Isle of Wight, Beachy Head and the South Downs, and the Weald to the north. The Ring was probably the capital of an Iron Age tribe, construction beginning before 300 BC using shovels made from animal shoulder blades and picks manufactured from deer antlers. Between 50 BC and AD 50, the site was abandoned.

From as early as 3,000 BC, this area was an industrial site, excavators digging as far down as 40 feet in the search for valuable flints, the industry surviving for over 1,000 years. Much prized, these flints were expertly fashioned into knives, scrapers, axe heads and arrow points, a lively trade developing; some items, according to the archaeological evidence, even finding their way to customers in the eastern Mediterranean. To this day, the area remains pockmarked with the depressions of over 250 flint pits, Cissbury being given the title 'The Sheffield of the Stone Age'.

Cissbury Ring was acquired by the National Trust in 1925, a public subscription raising the purchase price of £2,000.

Undisturbed for centuries, **this precious habitat** is colonised by a host of rare flowers including eight species of orchids and field fleawort (used in bedding by our ancient ancestors, being particularly effective against fleas and lice), the profusion attracting twenty-eight species of butterfly. The rarest of them all is the adonis blue. Adders, slow worms and lizards may also be seen.

There is a long forgotten legend associated with the site that will appeal to children. In the 1860s, there existed a 2 mile long, blocked-up tunnel from nearby **Offington Hall**. It led to the bowels of Cissbury wherein was said to lie a vast store of treasure. The owner of the hall promised half the treasure to any person who could clear the tunnel and several excavators began their laborious diggings only to be beaten back by a nest of serpents. The old hall was demolished ... but to this day, the treasure remains.

10
Balcombe

Walking the Planks

Walking the planks

O n an eminence surrounded by woods, the village of Balcombe overlooks the western arm of Ardingly Reservoir and it own pretty lake. This forest and fields amble leads us through woodland that once rang to the sound of forge hammers. On we go, over planks that would please any pirate, to the shore of Balcombe Lake, returning on a path skirting a cricket field.

◆ ◆

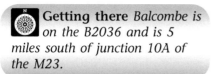 **Getting there** *Balcombe is on the B2036 and is 5 miles south of junction 10A of the M23.*

Length of walk 2½ miles.
Time 2½ hours.
Terrain Undulating field and forest paths, some using duck boards over boggy areas.
Start/Parking Park in the square outside the pub or on Bramble

Hill opposite the pub (GR 309307).
Map OS Explorer 135 Ashdown Forest.
Refreshments The Half Moon serves bar snacks and more substantial meals. Telephone: 01444 811582. The inviting Balcombe Tea Rooms on Bramble Hill (100 yards from the junction, on the right) offers light meals. Telephone: 01444 811777.

The Walk

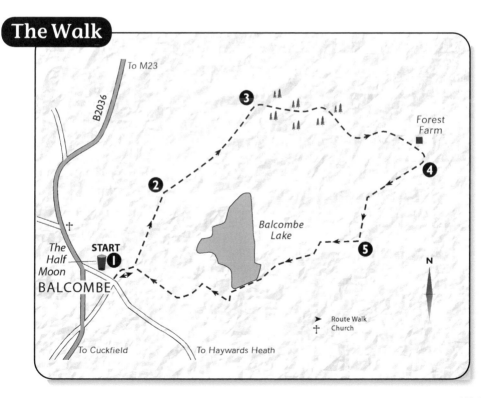

❶ Turn right away from the Half Moon and pass the Balcolmbe Stores. Swing right by Balcombe House to a signpost, going left through a gate into a meadow. Walk left of the big oak and follow the well-defined path left to a bi-directional sign, going right to a kissing gate. Go through. Drop down through woodland and keep on at the next sign, dropping down steps to the duck boards. Cross these and a bridge. Swing left.

❷ At the next signboard go right on a track for about $1/2$ mile, going through a gate and crossing a stone bridge. Walk forward from the bridge for 50 yards.

❸ Go right off the track, following a sign, crossing a planked bridge and duck boards. Swing left at the next signposts and walk between trees to a stile. Cross right, following a direction marker across a field to the corner. Then go diagonally right over the next field, following a path under the power lines to a stile by a gate. Cross and go left on a track. Cross a stile and keep forward at the signs, swinging left and merging with the access road to Forest Farm. Swing right on the access road for 100 yards.

❹ Go right, following a signpost down a hedgeline. Cross a stile in the field corner and go left,

◆ Fun Things to See and Do ◆

Ardingly Reservoir is about 3 miles southeast of Balcombe. Follow signs in Ardingley to reach this regional centre for water sports, offering dingy sailing, windsurfing, canoeing, rowing, power boating and coarse fishing from the Visitor Centre. Activities tend to be organised on a multi-session, pre-booked basis but 'taster' days for both children and adults are also available. Full details on **01444 892549**.

following a signpost to the next stile.

5 Cross and go hard right along a hedgeline. Cross the next stile and go left along the farm access road, dropping down right to the shore of Balcombe Lake. Go through the kissing gate right, following the sign, and go through the next kissing gate uphill to the hedge. Go left to the field corner. Turn right to the cricket field on a path. Steer right along the edge of the cricket field and go right on a track back to the starting point.

◆ Background Notes ◆

On the line of the Ouse Valley Railway, **Balcombe's viaduct**, built between 1839 and 1841, was one of the architectural and engineering wonders of Sussex. It has 37 arches and is 100 feet high and 500 yards in length. A nearby tunnel ran under Balcombe Forest where the famous scientist Dr Mantell of Lewes discovered the remains of an iguanodon.

There is still evidence of **iron working** in the forest, a number of discoloured, rusty pools pointing to the existence of age-old forge hammers and hammer ponds. The area was once known for its iron furnaces and its iron horses.

11
Climping

Beside the Seaside

Climping Beach.

Occupying a bend on the River Arun near Littlehampton, Climping is over a mile from its beach, which is the last undeveloped strip of virgin coastline on the stretch between Brighton and Bognor Regis. Now a nature reserve of shingle and sand, the area is the home of specialised plants such as sea kale and yellow horned poppy, its dunes and clean coastal waters providing a playground for children, windsurfers and jet skiers.

This walk over farmland paths and tracks delivers us to the beach, where you will find patches of sand suitable for youngsters.

Climping

 Getting there *Climping straddles the A259 just west of Littlehampton. Turn off the main road down Climping Street to the start of the walk.*

Length of walk 2½ miles.
Time 2 hours.
Terrain Flat tracks and footpaths but the shingle beach might pose difficulties for younger pedestrians.
Start/Parking There is a car park for customers at the Black Horse Inn (GR 003014) halfway down Climping Street as you approach from the A259, Crookthorne Lane, heading towards the sea. Please do seek permission, though, before leaving your car. Alternatively, use the private fee paying car park at the sea end of Climping Street in the Climping Beach Snack Bar's car park (open from the beginning of March until the end of September) and start the walk from Point 5.
Map OS Explorer 121 Arundel & Pulborough.
Refreshments The Black Horse Inn serves a good selection of steak and local fish dishes. It has a pleasant rear beer garden with country views. Telephone: 01903 715175. The Climping Beach Snack Bar at the end of Climping Street serves snacks in season.

◆ Fun Things to See and Do ◆

Windsurfing is a popular pastime at Climping Beach.

Three miles west down the A259 on the outskirts of Bognor Regis is **Butlins Resort**. Its compendium of family fun includes live entertainment, a fun fair, a swimming complex, go carts, a ten-pin bowling alley, a PC arena, a recording studio for kids and a Bob the Builder play centre. Family day tickets are available on selected (mainly weekday) dates between February and Christmas. Telephone: 01243 822445.

Kiddiwalks in West Sussex

◆◆*11*◆◆◆◆◆◆◆◆◆◆◆◆◆◆◆◆◆◆◆◆◆◆◆◆◆◆◆◆◆◆

The Walk

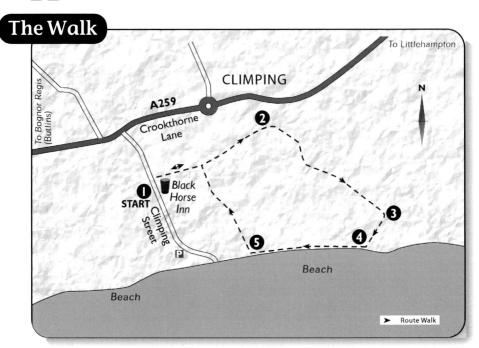

❶ Turn right along Climping Street from the inn for 150 yards. Go right again, following a footpath sign past the thatched cottages. Keep forward, crossing a field to an intersection of tracks. Go left, heading towards Kent's Farm, crossing a field to a barn.

❷ Turn 90 degrees right on a track for 50 yards and go forward at the bend, following a public footpath sign. Follow a hedgeline and swing right at the end of the hedge, crossing a field towards a wood. Cross a concrete bridge over

a ditch and swing left to a four-directional sign, keeping forward towards the middle of the wood. Cross a stile and enter the wood, following a public footpath sign. Walk along a winding path to the golf course.

❸ Turn right, following a public footpath sign to the West Beach Local Nature Reserve.

❹ Swing right on the shingle beach, passing the Second World War anti-tank blocks.

5 At the byway sign, turn right along the track. Keep going forward at the next sign and turn left on the outward route, back to the inn.

Will children discover the sign of the black horse?

◆ Background Notes ◆

To the north, **Climping village has an exquisite little church**. A famous litany to Sussex churches records: 'Bosham for antiquity; Boxgrove for beauty; Climping for perfection'. The church was partly built as a fortress to keep out marauding pirates.

12

East Dean

Trees and a Totem Pole

C lustered around a village pond, the wonderfully unspoilt East Dean exudes peace and tranquillity that defies the years. A luscious haven for relaxation over a quiet ginger beer, it has a delightful inn, a 12th century church and rows of old cottages bedecked with flowers in summertime.

Our ramble follows a sleepy rural lane into an equally quiet valley snuggled by high downs, our path leading through woodland and on to an unlikely encounter with a symbol of Red Indian culture that will have children calling for their tomahawks.

Getting there *East Dean is around 10 miles north-east of Chichester and can be accessed either from the A285 or the A286. The easiest route is from the A285 at Singleton, going east through Charlton.*

Length of walk 2¹/₂ miles.
Time 2 hours.
Terrain Quiet lanes with a little gradient and gently ascending/ descending field/woodland paths.
Start/Parking Park by the village pond and green (GR 903129).
Map OS Explorer 121 Arundel & Pulborough.
Refreshments The inviting Star and Garter in East Dean serves excellent bar and restaurant meals, specialising in fresh seafood. It has its own shellfish bar and an attractive beer garden. Telephone: 01243 811318.

◆ Fun Things to See and Do ◆

West's of East Dean (on our route) make everything from totem poles to grandfather clocks and a visit to their showrooms is interesting even for young children. Ask to see the inscribed section of a yew tree salvaged from a specimen blown down in the great gale. Its annual rings are cleverly employed as a calendar to give dramatic visual effect to the unfolding of British history. Telephone: 01243 811354.

Nearby in Singleton on the A286 is England's leading museum of historic buildings and traditional rural life, its collection encompassing over 45 structures rescued from destruction. The **Weald & Downland Open Air Museum** is set in a beautiful 50 acre downland setting, with exhibits including a medieval farmstead, a working 17th century watermill, a functioning Tudor kitchen, demonstrations of traditional rustic skills and groups of shire horses and farm animals. Open daily March to October. Restricted opening during the winter months. Telephone: 01243 811348.

The Walk

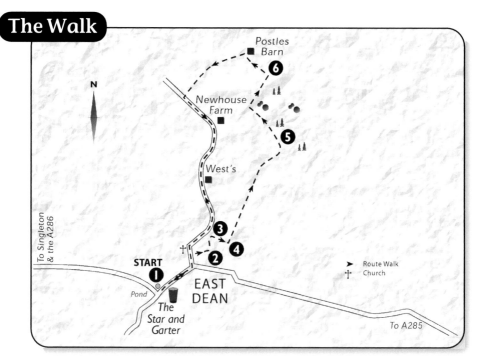

❶ Walk past the chapel and the pub up the lane up to the bus shelter.

❷ Go left on Newhouse Lane for 100 yards and turn right, following a public bridleway sign. Go left by the bungalow called Hebron and swing right on Newhouse Lane.

❸ Turn right, following a public footpath sign to the field corner.

❹ Go left on a woodland fringed track and walk up to the Charlton Forest sign.

❺ Go left on a track. At the tri-directional sign, turn right, following the public bridleway and dropping down.

❻ Swing left to the gate and go through on a track, swinging left and merging with Newhouse Lane. Pass Newhouse Farm and the West's furniture workshop and showroom, noting the totem pole. Keep on to the bus shelter and turn right back to the starting point.

The workshops where totem poles are made nestle in the countryside (photo courtesy of L. West & Son, East Dean).

◆ Background Notes ◆

East Dean is really off the tourist trail and it is totally unspoilt. It is one of the best places in the county to see the traditional craft of building in flint. Its rows of cottages and its dreamy 12th century church on the edge of the village have some particularly fine examples.

13

St Leonard's Forest

If You Go Down in the Woods Today

The forest is a valuable sanctuary for wildlife.

B esieged on all sides, a million trunks stand in resolute defiance of the ground-hungry assaults of modern man, the vast wilderness that was the ancient St Leonard's Forest now being reduced to a few hundred precious acres. Thankfully, though, someone has drawn a line in the sand and this precious oasis, sandwiched between two major roads and the metropolises of Crawley and Horsham, survives and is being appreciated and cared for by the Forestry Commission.

This lovely walk takes you into the heart of the forest, the intermingling smells of pine and heather, the magnificent sights of armies of specimen trees, the cool shade on hot days, the opportunities to see and hear rare birds such as the nightjar and the sheer sense of peace adding to a sensory experience that is more pronounced for the fact that the forest is just a few miles south of the busyness of Gatwick.

And St Leonard's Forest is the legendary home of the saint of the same name ... and a rather repulsive beast that regularly drew his blood!

St Leonard's Forest

Getting there *St Leonard's Forest is about 5 miles south-west of Crawley between the A23 and the A24 just east of Horsham. The easiest access to the starting point is along the A281 between Mannings Heath and Horsham. Turn off northwards on Doomsday Lane (just east of the Hornbrook Inn) and then right, going down and up hill for about a mile to the signposted parking area at Roosthole.*

Length of walk 2³/₄ miles.
Time 2¹/₂ hours.

Terrain Largely flat forest tracks and paths – occasional boggy patches.
Start/Parking Start at the signposted free Forestry Commission Roosthole car park (GR 206297).
Map OS Explorer 134 Crawley & Horsham.
Refreshments The Hornbrook Inn (back along Doomsday Lane and turn right). It serves good quality bar meals and daily specials. Telephone: 01403 252638.

◆ Fun Things to See and Do ◆

Holmbush Farm World at Faygate between Horsham and Crawley (north of St Leonard's Forest on the A264) enables young children to encounter farm animals at close quarters. The farm organises goat races – children can compete – and it also has play equipment and a maze. Telephone: 01293 851000.

Kiddiwalks in West Sussex

◆◆*13*◆◆◆◆◆◆◆◆◆◆◆◆◆◆◆◆◆◆◆◆◆◆◆◆◆◆◆◆◆◆◆

The Walk

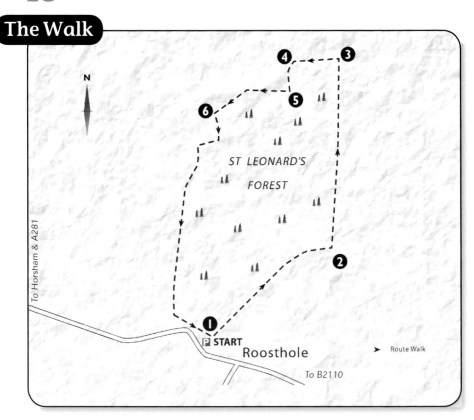

❶ Take the broad forest access road opposite the car park and walk on for just over ¹/₂ mile, swinging right to a bridleway sign.

❷ Go left on an intersecting access road for just under ³/₄ mile, following the sign 'High Weald Landscape Trail'. Keep forward at the four-direction sign and watch out for the next unsigned track left.

❸ Turn left.

❹ Turn left again.

❺ Turn right and walk on to the area currently undergoing heathland restoration (information board to the right).

❻ Go left at the fork and swing left downhill to the next footpath sign. Go right and next left, passing through the low-lying area known as the Lily Beds. Turn right on the next track and go left down the steps using the handrails. Swing right over the duck boards, going left, right and right again back to the car park.

◆ Background Notes ◆

With help from local colleges of volunteers (known as Green Gymnasts!), **the Forestry Commission is reclaiming the forest**. Non-native species of trees are being systematically removed and replaced with indigenous varieties and pockets of age-old heathland are being restored in an internationally important programme to encourage the growth of heather and the establishment of rare creatures such as the nightjar, adder and silver studded blue butterfly.

St Leonard's Forest was described in 1614 as 'a vast and unfrequented place, heathie, vaultie, full of unwholesome shades and overgrowne hollowes' where a nine feet long serpent or dragon lived. Such was the beast's stench that people and animals dropped down dead! On the positive side, it preferred rabbits to human flesh. **St Leonard** tried to slay the dragon on his frequent visits to the forest but without success. The saint was often injured in the encounters, his blood giving rise to the miraculous blossoming of lilies of the valley, these flowers adorning the springtime glades to this day.

The forest area was once exploited for its **iron ore deposits** and traces of ironstone can still be found on some stream banks.

The **Arun,** the largest river in Sussex, rises in St Leonard's Forest.

14

Cocking

Climbing up the Downs

The track into Cocking.

A t the foot of Cocking Hill, in a break in the northern escarpment of the South Downs, the busy village of Cocking is surrounded by hills planted with dense woods and pockmarked by tumuli and burial mounds. A district of swirling contours, it is a favourite haunt of buzzards and other raptors, this quite challenging walk, up Sun Combe onto Manorfarm Down, giving you eagle-eyed views. Part of our route returns along the spectacular South Downs Way, a track fluttered by hundreds of butterflies in summer.

Cocking

Getting there *Cocking is 2 miles south of Midhurst on the A286.*

Length of walk 2³/₄ miles.
Time 3 hours.
Terrain Field and woodland

paths and farm tracks, some overgrown (long trousers recommended). One very steep ascent through woodland at the beginning of the walk precludes children under about 10 years old.

◆ Fun Things to See and Do ◆

The imaginative and beautifully executed **Cocking Millennium Obelisk** depicts the history of the village and the nation in a series of wrap-around bronze reliefs. Children will enjoy straining their necks to see the figures engaged in compulsory archery practice in 1150, the wretched people suffering from the famine of 1340, and the boy who blew up the village cross with explosives! The obelisk is at the corner of a field, 100 yards south of Moonlight Cottage Tearooms and turning right along an access track for 100 yards.

The local Cowdray Estate is famed as the home of British **polo**. International matches are staged during the season between April and October. Children under 12 have free entry. Telephone: 01730 812423.

Petworth Park, around 7 miles east of Midhurst on the A272, is a magnificent National Trust mansion set in a 700 acre deer park. Children will particularly enjoy its extensive servants' quarters, the 'below stairs' tour and quizzes. Telephone: 01798 342207.

Kiddiwalks in West Sussex

◆◆ *14* ◆◆◆◆◆◆◆◆◆◆◆◆◆◆◆◆◆◆◆◆◆◆◆◆◆◆◆

Start/Parking The Blue Bell has a car park for customers, please ask permission from the landlord before leaving your car (GR 878175), or you could leave your car down side lanes.
Map Explorer 120 Chichester, South Harting & Selsey.
Refreshments Moonlight Cottage Tearooms on the A286 serves light lunches and snacks. Telephone: 01730 813336. Also on the main road is the Blue Bell, which has a pleasant beer garden to the side. The food includes fresh salads, pasta dishes and fresh fish, and there is a separate menu for children. Telephone: 01730 813449.

The Walk

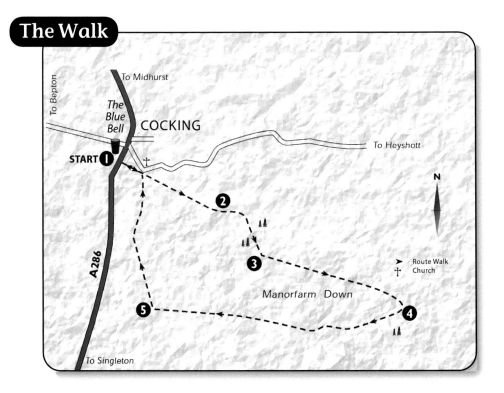

Cocking's millennium obelisk.

Kiddiwalks in West Sussex

14 ◆◆◆◆◆◆◆◆◆◆◆◆◆◆◆◆◆◆◆◆◆◆◆◆

❶ From the Blue Bell, cross the road and go right. Turn left down Church Lane to the white war memorial outside the church and, facing southeast, go left on the lane for 100 yards and right up the steps to a stile and a footpath sign. Cross a field to the edge of a wood. At the big ash tree, go left (sign overgrown) and follow the yellow arrow marker on a post. Swing right, following the woodland edge, climbing up steeply to a gate and a bi-directional sign.

❷ Go through right into the wood, following the sign, and climb a steep woodland path to a stile.

❸ Go left across the field, following a footpath sign to a stile. Cross left, heading for the top right hand corner of the wood across the large field. Keep left in the middle of the field and merge with a stony track. Head up left of where the two woods converge. Swing right near the tree house to a five-directional sign.

❹ Turn right on a track along the South Downs Way and drop down to a gate. Proceed forward to the tri-directional sign.

❺ Turn right past the barn and drop down a sunken-hedged track towards Cocking. Swing right to rejoin the outward route and go left back to the war memorial and the church.

◆ **Background Notes** ◆

Cocking is a large and once important village of Saxon origin. It had 5 mills and was a centre for industry and agriculture.

There is a **local weather saying**, 'Foxes Brew', describing a mist which portends rain. When it rolls down from the woods like 'a snake from a chimney' it's time to raise your umbrella.

15
Arundel

Kings of the Castle

Boating on Swanbourne Lake.

Asplendid little town, just 4 miles from the sea, Arundel wears its castle like a crown, one of the most sumptuous private residences in the entire kingdom, setting the gold standard for the network of lovely old streets, courtyards and buildings that huddle at its feet and overlook one of the largest rivers in Sussex.

This regal walk takes us to the castle entrance and through its palatial parkland grounds to a hushed and beautiful valley, the route passing a fabulous lake painted by the famous artists Turner, Constable, Prout and Vicat Cole. In a grand finale, the path leads us along the banks of the River Arun with grandstand views of the castle all the way.

Kiddiwalks in West Sussex

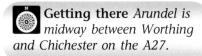

15

Getting there *Arundel is midway between Worthing and Chichester on the A27.*

Length of walk 2³/₄ or 3¹/₂ miles.
Time 3¹/₂ hours or 4 hours for the longer route.

Terrain One fairly steep ascent up the High Street into Arundel and then gently undulating field paths and tracks concluding with a looping saunter along the Arun banks.
Start/Parking Park in the pay and display Fitzalan Pool car

◆ Fun Things to See and Do ◆

Arundel Castle is obviously the main attraction. This ancestral home of the Dukes of Norfolk and their ancestors for over 850 years is the repository for priceless collections of art and furniture. Events include historical re-enactments and falconry displays. The castle is open from April until the end of October but is closed every Saturday except on Bank Holiday weekends. Telephone: 01903 883136/882173.

Castle Trout Feeding Pond (at point 5 on the walk) gives youngsters the opportunity to feed trout at close quarters.

Rowing boats may be hired on **Swanbourne Lake** – telephone: 01903 884293 – and duck food can be purchased lakeside.

Nearly at the end of our walk, motor boats can be hired and river excursions taken from the **Arundel Boatyard and River Cruises** wharf. Telephone: 01903 882609.

The popular **open air heated swimming pool** – a main pool and children's pool in one of the most beautiful locations in England – is open in season and is conveniently located beside the parking area. Telephone: 01903 882404.

The Walk

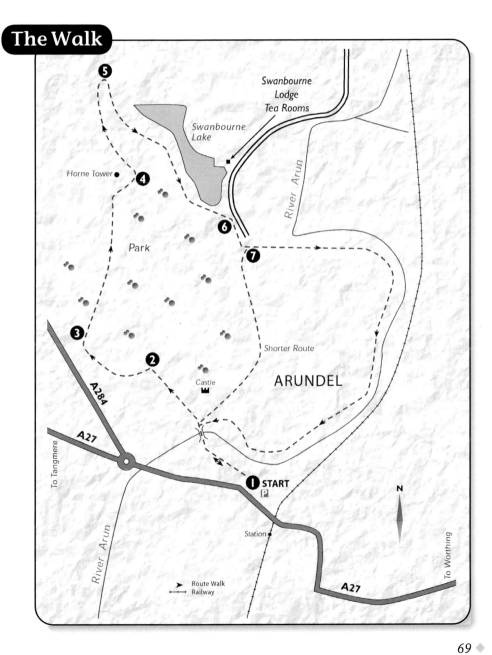

Swanbourne
Lodge
Tea Rooms

⑤

Swanbourne
Lake

River Arun

Horne Tower ● **④**

⑥

⑦

Park

③

Shorter Route

②

Castle

ARUNDEL

A284

A27

To Tangmere

River Arun

① START
🅿

N

Station ●

To Worthing

A27

➤ Route Walk
├──┤ Railway

Kiddiwalks in West Sussex

park (GR 021069). To reach this, take the 'Town Centre' route off the roundabout near Arundel Station and turn right.
Map OS Explorer 121 Arundel & Pulborough.
Refreshments On our route, snacks, light meals and cream teas are served at Swanbourne Lodge Tea Rooms. Telephone: 01903 884293. In the town, Arundel has lots of quality hotels, pubs, cafés and restaurants to suit every pocket.

❶ Go to the far end of the car park, climb the riverbank and go left through a gate. Swing left away from the bank and go immediately right, following a 'Castle and Town Centre' sign on top of a parking post, through an alley. Turn right to the bridge and cross the river, going straight forward on High Street, uphill to the castle.

❷ Go left by the entrance and continue past the cathedral, walking on to a lane and a gatehouse.

The Horne Tower in Arundel Park.

❸ Turn right, following a public footpath sign, on a driveway into Arundel Park (access denied on 24th March each year). Go straight forward through the gates into the parkland and walk on to a point about 100 yards before Horne Tower. Turn right off the

◆ Background Notes ◆

There was **a fortress in Arundel** long before the Norman Conquest but 1066 witnessed the arrival of a new lord, Roger Montgomery becoming the first Earl of Arundel as a prize for his assistance at Hastings. The castle took a pounding during the English Civil War but was only partially repaired until the closing years of the 18th century when the 10th Duke executed a complete restoration. During the last 25 years of his life, hundreds of workmen completed the task.

Above the castle gateway is the **figure of a lion** whose origin springs from an old legend. In a joust in Paris, the Earl of Arundel so distinguished himself that the Queen of France fell in love with him, desiring his hand in marriage. He refused, saying he was already betrothed to another lady, the rejection causing the queen to lock him in a cave and release a lion to gobble him up. As brave as ever, the earl boxed its ears and pulled out its tongue, commemorating the act in a sculpture to adorn the entrance to his Sussex home.

Children will be interested in the castle's **Bevis Tower**, history suggesting that it was built for the use of Bevis of Hampton, a brave and mighty giant whose weekly appetite could only be sated with two barrels of beer, a whole ox and masses of bread and mustard. Bevis possessed *Morglay* – a magical sword – and he owned a marvellously gifted horse called *Hirondelle*. The giant was so big that he could wade between his home and the Isle of Wight without getting his chest wet! When he was about to die, he climbed his tower and cast *Morglay* a great distance, instructing his attendants to bury him where his blade fell. He now lies under a mound with his sword in a valley called Pugh Dean. *Morglay* is reputed to have never rusted and waits to be found! (See also walks 1 and 8.)

Swanbourne Lake was originally a mill pond, the long demolished mill featuring in several well known paintings. The lake is over 1,000 years old. It is now a Site of Special Scientific Interest and is home to tawny owls, nightingales, woodpeckers, tufted ducks and four kinds of bat.

drive and over the turf, following a yellow arrow marker, to find a gap in the hedge and a footpath sign.

4 Go left on a track downhill and through a gate, dropping down into the bottom.

5 Go right down the floor of the valley and cross a stile by a gate. Go right and swing left, passing Swanbourne Lake. Keep on the track and exit onto a lane by a trout farm (Swanbourne Lodge is a short distance left).

6 Go right and cross the bridge. (The shorter route may be completed by keeping forward here along the tree-lined Mill Road back to the outward bridge.)

7 For the longer route, turn left and go right across a stile, walking down the old cut to the river. Follow the winding bank right back to the outward bridge and go left back to the starting point.

Sparrowhawk.

16

Guildenhurst (near Billingshurst)

A Lost Route to the Sea

I t must have been a spree being an old bargee! This delightful ramble leads us along the lazy curves of one of their long abandoned river canals that at one time linked the wharves of London with the English Channel. You can almost hear the chug-chug of the *Sussex Pride* and smell her master's pipe as you follow the bends to Lording's Lock where you will discover a marvellous revival underway. Thanks to a dedicated team of enthusiastic volunteers, the Wey and Arun Junction Canal is beginning to live again. Its banks abound with waterside flowers and wildlife of every description, our route using part of the long distance Wey-South Path and returning along the shoreline of a beautiful lake.

Kiddiwalks in West Sussex

Getting there
Guildenhurst is 1 mile west of Billingshurst (A29). Go west from the village, crossing two roundabouts keeping the same direction, and turn second left along the B2133 for 250 yards to the Limeburners.

Length of walk 3 miles.
Time 3 hours.
Terrain Fairly flat canal, river, field and woodland paths. Some are overgrown in places and long trousers are recommended.
Start/Parking The Limeburners has a car park for customers (GR 074254). Alternatively, you could leave your car alongside the B2133. If leaving your car in the pub car park, please seek permission from the staff.
Map OS Explorer 134 Crawley and Horsham.
Refreshments The Limeburners. This attractive roadside hostelry has a fascinating history. It began life as a row of three lime-workers' cottages at New Bridge Wharf on the Wey and Arun Canal. The row was relocated here when the canal closed and was converted for use as a pub. It serves good bar meals including fresh fish and has a pleasant beer garden and a children's play area. Telephone: 01403 782311. Meals are also available at Fisher's Farm Park (see 'Fun Things to See and Do') in the Farmers Grill and the Farm Barn Restaurant. Telephone: 01403 700063.

◆ Fun Things to See and Do ◆

Fisher's Farm Park at Wisborough Green – just north of Guildenhurst along the B2133 and left down Newpound Lane – is an award winning adventure park for 2–12 year-old children, offering multiple attractions including a climbing wall, tractor, combine harvester and pony rides, quad bikes, indoor play barns, adventure golf, bumper boats, a helter-skelter and a ghost train. Open all year. Telephone: 01403 700063.

The Walk

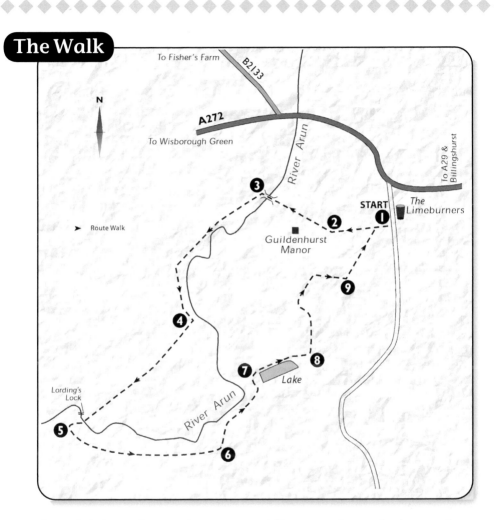

❶ Go left from the inn for 150 yards along the lane and turn right along the lane signed 'Guildenhurst Manor'. Walk forward almost to the manor entrance drive.

❷ Turn right over a stile, following a footpath sign, and cross a meadow right to a second stile left of a gate. Cross and walk over the next meadow to a third stile and cross, going right, following a signpost downhill to a bridge over the canal. Cross.

Kiddiwalks in West Sussex

16

❸ Go left and keep forward to a stile. Cross and keep forward to large field.

❹ Go right hedgeside, heading away from the canal. Swing right at the end of the field then swing left to find a hidden signpost and cross a stile, going right to the Lording's Lock restoration. *The newly erected waterwheel here is thought to be unique in the whole national canal system. River flow turns the wheel, which will deliver water to the restored lock.* Walk down the lock side.

❺ Go left over the bridge and follow the footpath, swinging left through a gate and climbing a gentle slope to a bi-directional sign, going left.

❻ At the top of the rise, go left, following the signpost, through a copse to the river. Go right. Cross a stile and follow the riverbank. Go left over the footbridge.

❼ Turn right by the lake, following the footpath sign to the boathouse.

❽ Turn left uphill and keep left of the big barn. Go left at the marker post by the next barn and go right, following the signs over a planked bridge. Walk on by the side of a railed fence and go right at the corner to the next corner.

❾ Go left, following the signs, and (ignoring the broad track right) keep straight forward, going through a small gate and heading diagonally right across a field. Go through a gate and forward to a kissing gate, going through and right, back onto the outward route, to return to the start.

◆ Background Notes ◆

Using the **Wey and Arun Junction Canal**, the distance by canal from London Bridge to Lording's Lock was 67 miles. The canal was built between 1785 and 1816. It was 23 miles long with 26 locks, providing a vital link between the national waterways system and the English Channel. It also joined Surrey and Sussex to the network. The canal, known as 'London's Lost Route to the Sea', was closed in 1888 and finally abandoned in 1896 but is now being lovingly restored by a dedicated team of volunteers for the benefit of wildlife and the enjoyment of future generations. Lording's was the summit lock.

17
Ardingly
Sailing Along

A tribute to a former windsurfing instructor at Ardingly.

O n a plateau overlooking the pretty Ardingly Brook and Shell Brook, the ancient, formerly largely agricultural village of Ardingly, was transformed during the 1970s when its waters were confined to create a nature reserve and one of the most exciting centres for water sports in the South East.

This scenic walk takes you from the venerable St Peter's church on a downward path to the shoreline and on to the Visitor Centre hard by the dam wall. The return route is through fields giving long-distance views of the surrounding countryside.

Kiddiwalks in West Sussex

17

Getting there *Ardingly is 4 miles north of Haywards Heath on the B2028.*

Length of walk 3 miles.
Time 3 hours.
Terrain Field tracks and a waterside path. The uphill return route through fields is overgrown in places and long trousers are recommended.
Start/Parking Take the Balcombe road – Street Lane – through the village, going north-west from the B2028 junction for ¹/₂ mile, passing the Oak pub and the school. Park 50 yards left off this road down Church Lane (GR 339298); 2 spaces available near the side entrance to St Peter's church adjacent to the rectory access. Alternatively, park 100 yards back from the church on Street Lane in the layby opposite the school.
Map OS Explorer 135 Ashdown Forest.
Refreshments The flower-decked Oak in Ardingly village is an attractive roadside inn dating from the early 17th century. It offers popular pies and roast lunches, and welcomes children. Telephone: 01444 892244.

The Walk

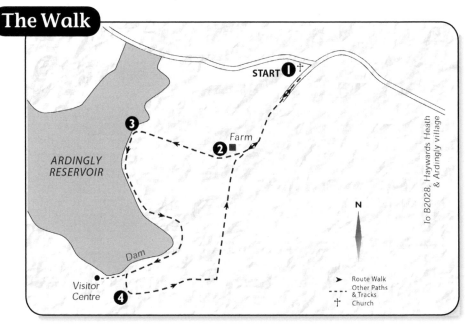

❶ Walk away from the church down Church Lane. Swing right at Old Knowles Cottages on a track, following the public footpath sign.

❷ At the path junction at Townhouse Farm, follow the four-directional sign right, walking along a hedgeside path, crossing stiles to the reservoir bank.

❸ Turn left bankside, following the public footpath sign. Continue to the kissing gate. *There is a bird hide on your right. Local species include grebes, mallards, Canada geese, kingfishers, reed warblers and ospreys.* Swing right over the dam to the Visitor Centre.

❹ About face and head diagonally right downhill towards the car park. Go left, following a public footpath sign, and go right over a stile, following the direction marker through the new

◆ Fun Things to See and Do ◆

Ardingly is a regional centre for water sports, offering dingy sailing, windsurfing, canoeing, rowing, power boating and coarse fishing from the Visitor Centre, which we visit on this walk. Activities tend to be organised on a multi-session, pre-booked course basis but 'taster' days for both children and adults are also available. Full details on 01444 892549.

Around 2 miles east of Ardingly is **Horsted Keynes Station** on the steam-hauled Bluebell Railway. Children will enjoy the smoke and sparks of an atmospheric ride to Sheffield Park (southern terminus) and Kingscote (northern terminus) stations. In June each year, the railway hosts Thomas the Tank Engine weekends. Both Thomas and Percy attend in 'puffson' together with Sir Topham Hatt (the Fat Controller), additional entertainment including Punch and Judy and magic shows, clowns and roundabouts. Advance tickets on 01825 720831. The railway also organises Santa Specials. Advance tickets on 01825 720806. Timetable Telephone: 01825 720825.

Kiddiwalks in West Sussex

plantation. Swing right and go immediately left to the next sign, going right over a stile to a field. Keep left of the power lines and go forward uphill, continuing hedgeside to the next sign. Fork right into a wood and cross a stile, going right and following a fieldside path. Cross the next stile and keep forward at the side of the cottages, swinging left to the outward four-directional sign. Turn right back along the outward route to the start.

Kids old and young will enjoy a ride to Sheffield Park.

◆ Background Notes ◆

Ardingly is an important water storage reservoir providing surplus flows released into the Ouse river in times of drought. Flows are intercepted and stored in turn in Barcombe Reservoir near Lewes before being treated for onward distribution to thousands of customers in mid-Sussex. The reservoir has been nurtured as a vital habitat for wildlife and is designated as a Local Nature Reserve. Endangered dormice are known to frequent its woodland areas and magnificent ospreys visit the area every August and September during their migrations from Scotland en route to the over-wintering grounds in Africa. Identification boards in the bird hide are helpful in recognising the reservoir's other visitors. South East Water has published two leaflets about the reservoir and its activities. Both are available free of charge from the Visitor Centre.

Located in the village, **Ardingly College** is a world famous public school.

18
West Wittering

Splashdown!

Marvellous wide open spaces at West Wittering.

N ear the far flung western extremity of West Sussex overlooking the vast tidal expanse of sand and mudflats known as Chichester Harbour, West Wittering may have been the first landfall of the Roman legions in 55 BC. People have been coming to its yawning beach ever since, its precious East Head sand dunes owned by the National Trust being regarded as one of the last bastions of natural coastal sand dunes in the county.

This energetic and enlivening walk steers clear of the usual tourist route to the beach, treading the interesting path of ancient pilgrims who came to pray at the shrine of a local saint. It continues over a creek where a purpose-built children's Crab Pool will engage the little ones for hours. Onward then over a causeway to the dunes and the beach, returning along the creek edge and through the village back to the start.

Kiddiwalks in West Sussex

◆ ◆ *18* ◆

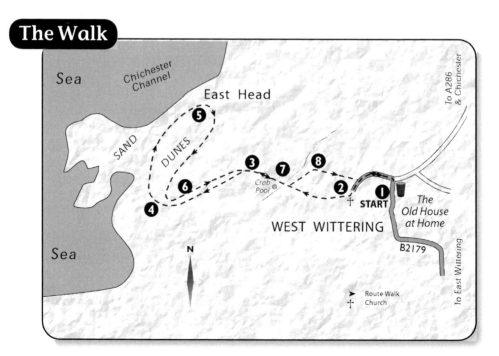

Getting there *West Wittering is about 8 miles south-west of Chichester. Take the A286 to Birdham and keep straight on along the B2179 until you reach the Old House at Home pub.*

Length of walk 3 miles.
Time 3 hours.
Terrain Flat and level lanes and field paths, a beach and sand dunes (with a board walk).
Start/Parking There is a car park for customers at the Old House at Home on the bend in Cakeham Road, West Wittering (GR 779984) or you could opt for on-street parking but see 'Background Notes'.
Map OS Explorer 120 Chichester, South Harting & Selsey.
Refreshments The attractive Old House at Home offers bar and restaurant meals and is particularly noted for fresh fish. It has a pleasant beer garden to the rear. Telephone: 01243 511234.

The Walk

Sea

Chichester Channel

East Head

To A286 & Chichester

SAND DUNES

⑤

③ **⑦** **⑧**

Crab Pool

⑥ **②**

④ ✝ **START** The Old House at Home

WEST WITTERING

B2179

Sea

N

To East Wittering

➤ Route Walk
✝ Church

❶ Turn right from the Old House at Home and go left on the lane signposted to West Wittering Beach. Pass the private road entrance to the left and keep straight on along the cul-de-sac lane. Swing left to the church of St Peter and St Paul.

❷ Go right through the churchyard and leave through a gap in the wall, dropping down steps, and cross a field, heading towards a caravan park. Go through a gate and walk through the park then go right along a private road, following a public footpath sign. Swing right and go left, following a public footpath sign, and left again at Snow Hill to the Crab Pool.

❸ Swing left on the causeway to reach the beach.

❹ Swing right and go north, walking on the sands to East Head.

❺ Weave right into the sand dunes and pick up a track. Continue on a raised causeway, ignoring the left turns, proceeding back to the end of point 3.

❻ Turn left, this time walking left of and beneath the causeway at the side of the creek. Go up the steps and walk on the causeway back to the Crab Pool.

❼ Go left at the tri-directional sign for 250 yards.

❽ Turn right at the four-directional sign, going through a gate, and keep on continuing straight forward through a kissing

◆ Fun Things to See and Do ◆

There is only one thing to do in this wonderful playground of sky and sea. Head down to **X-Train** in West Wittering, dude, for windsurfing, kitesurfing and power boating. Specialist kids' windsurfing courses for ages 5 plus. Telephone: 01243 513077; website: www.x-train.co.uk

Enjoying the crab pool.

gate, following a public footpath sign towards the church. Go through a second kissing gate and continue forward to the lane. Go right and left on the outward route, back to the start.

◆ Background Notes ◆

Parking in the very popular West Wittering can be a particular problem during the busy summer months. The lack of parking is exploited by a local landowner who has private ownership of part of West Wittering beach and one of its main access roads (see point 1). Motorists are charged exorbitant parking fees. If you want to leave your car in the Old House at Home car park while you walk, do remember to notify staff first otherwise you may well be wheel clamped.

In the Chapel of Our Lady and St Richard is a tomb to a boy bishop (the only other in England is in Salisbury). In the Middle Ages it was a custom to elect a boy bishop for ceremonial installation three weeks before Christmas, the boy being properly robed and mitred and treated like a proper bishop. It would appear that this one died 'in office'. There are as many as forty crosses scratched into the stonework pillar at the back of the chapel. They may be the marks of pilgrims who came seeking the intercession of St Richard, Richard Wych, Bishop of Chichester between 1245 and 1253 who was canonised in 1262. He had a country retreat in West Wittering, Cakeham Manor, whose Tudor tower is still a local landmark. The carved tomb cover on a low table to the left of the altar may have adorned his sacred remains.

The **Crab Pool** at the end of point 2 on the walk was established following suggestions by children and their parents for a safe and easy place to catch small crustaceans and fish. It has concreted banks and a bench for adults.

Bathing is not recommended as a consequence of the strong tidal currents hereabouts but the tide leaves some **safe paddle-depth pools**, which can be safely enjoyed by even the youngest children.

The strand hereabouts is a **geological treasure trove**, yielding specimen boulders of such erratics as granite, gneiss and basalt deposited during the last Ice Age.

Woolbeding Common (near Redford)

Left Right! Left Right Left!

The heady view at Woolbeding Common.

I n an area of outstanding natural beauty this National Trust gem is the most scintillating treasure of all, its amphitheatre of forest, gorse and heather inhabited by rare birds like stonechat, Dartford warbler and nightjar, providing a unique walking experience enhanced by some of the best views in the county.

This challenging walk (more for its frequent changes of direction than harsh terrain) is for the most part through woodland and a low-lying area known as Stedham Marsh, which is used by local schools for field trips and nature study.

Woolbeding Common (near Redford)

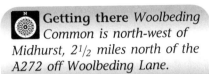 **Getting there** *Woolbeding Common is north-west of Midhurst, 2¹/₂ miles north of the A272 off Woolbeding Lane.*

Length of walk 3 miles.
Time 3 hours.
Terrain Quiet lanes at the start and finish but largely woodland paths with one gradual and one steep ascent. The well-signposted route involves lots of changes of direction. Suitable for budding orienteers (buy them compasses for Christmas!). After rain the tracks can be muddy in places.
Start/Parking Park in the designated National Trust car park (GR 869260) – take the dead-end lane off Woolbeding Lane/Linch Road.
Map OS Explorer Haslemere & Petersfield.
Refreshments There are no facilities for refreshments on this walk. Bring a picnic and enjoy a feast in tremendous scenery from the bench referred to at the end of point 8 in the walk directions.

◆ Fun Things to See and Do ◆

 The local Cowdray Estate is famed as the home of British **polo**. International matches are staged during the season between April and October. Children under 12 have free entry. Telephone: 01730 812423.

Petworth Park, around 7 miles east of Midhurst on the A272, is a magnificent National Trust mansion set in a 700 acre deer park. Children will particularly enjoy its extensive servants' quarters, the 'below stairs' tour and quizzes. Telephone: 01798 342207.

19

The Walk

❶ Turn left from the car park, and walk along the access lane.

❷ Take the next signed footpath right and go down to Linch Road.

❸ Cross left over the open ground and go left, following the public footpath sign to the tri-directional sign. Go right, dropping down into the wood to the four-directional sign. Cross the track and keep forward, swinging right to a tri-directional sign near the fenced clearing ahead. Go right towards the clearing corner.

❹ Go left at the blue arrow marker along the clearing edge and swing left on a track along the edge of the next fenced clearing.

❺ At the next tri-directional sign go right and continue, following the green arrow markers to Titty Hill.

Woolbeding Common (near Redford)

◆◆◆◆◆◆◆◆◆◆◆◆◆◆◆◆◆◆◆◆◆◆◆◆◆◆◆◆◆◆

❻ Turn right on a track for 50 yards and go right, following the yellow arrow marker on a post. Keep straight on at the next two tri-directional signs and swing right by the edge of the fenced clearing to the four-directional sign. Swing left at the edge of the clearing and continue to Linch Road and the hamlet of Redford.

❼ Walk up the metalled lane for 150 yards to the tri-directional sign and follow the lane signposted to Hookland.

❽ At the next tri-directional sign turn right and walk up to the yellow arrow marker on a post. Go left uphill, swinging right to the four-directional post near Barnett's Cottage. Swing left, passing the cottage log stores, uphill to the next tri-directional sign by the log seat. Keep forward and climb steeply to the crest by the bench. *This is a good place for your picnic.*

❾ Turn right along the lane back to the car park.

◆ Background Notes ◆

South of Woolbeding Common, in a loop of the River Rother, is the little hamlet of **Woolbeding**, the National Trust also owning a beautiful linear wood along the riverbank. As its name suggests the area was once noted for its fleeces, the production of wool supporting the weaving industry in nearby Midhurst. Woolbeding has a delightful old church and an ancient manor house.

20
Amberley Station

River Prance

Tramcar at Amberley Working Museum.

etached from its village, Amberley Station overlooks the
serpentine Arun, the lusciously loopy, gently flowing river
guiding us on a relaxing walk along banks high with reeds to
the soporific hamlets of North and South Stoke. Bring a cushion!

In the old days, the Arun was prone to regular flooding and the
residents of Amberley were once described as 'web-footed', its female
residents having 'yellow bellies' from the practice of lifting their skirts
and warming themselves over smoky fires. Amberley Swamp and the
flood plain north of the village known as Amberley Wild Brooks are still
ideal for ducks but a network of drainage ditches and embankments
and reduced rainfall allows pedestrians to ramble elsewhere dry-shod.

The walk sets out from the gracefully spanned and ancient Houghton
Bridge, a series of raised causeways and footbridges taking us over ings
land, the watery habitat encouraging the lush growth of rare waterside
plants, these in turn attracting many attractive birds such as warblers
and herons. Part of the return route upstream is through delightful
woodland carpeted in ferns.

◆◆◆◆◆◆◆◆◆◆◆◆◆◆◆◆◆◆◆◆◆◆◆◆◆◆◆◆◆◆◆◆◆◆◆

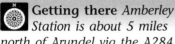 **Getting there** *Amberley Station is about 5 miles north of Arundel via the A284 and the B2139, going north-east through Houghton.*

Length of walk 3³/₄ miles.
Time 4 hours.
Terrain Flat, riverside and fieldside paths, some of which can be muddy after rain.
Start/Parking Parking can be difficult around Amberley Station and the constricted Houghton Bridge. If you intend to visit Amberley Working Museum (and I would wholeheartedly recommend that you do) the easiest arrangement is to pay first (see 'Fun Things to See and Do') and park in their extensive private car park. There is an adjacent toilet. Alternatively, if you are intending to use the closely-clustered facilities of the Bridge Inn or the Houghton Bridge Riverside Tea Garden and Restaurant, park in one of their car parks, but do ask permission first. (GR 027118 – starting point at Amberley Station.)
Map OS Explorer 121 Arundel & Pulborough.

◆ Fun Things to See and Do ◆

True to its name, the **Amberley Working Museum** is action all the way. Covering 36 acres of a former chalk pit complex with 38 separate attractions – you need at least half a day to explore – it imaginatively recreates village and town scenes of long ago. But unlike other museums with their glass cases and simulations, there is nothing static or contrived here, old buses chugging between stops, engines and machinery rattling and steaming and craftsmen and women producing everything from clay pipes to walking sticks. The museum has a narrow gauge railway, a children's playground, a gift shop and a restaurant. The museum, which is open between March and October, was the location for the James Bond movie *A View to a Kill*. Telephone: 01798 831370.

◆◆20◆◆◆◆◆◆◆◆◆◆◆◆◆◆◆◆◆◆◆◆◆◆◆

The Walk

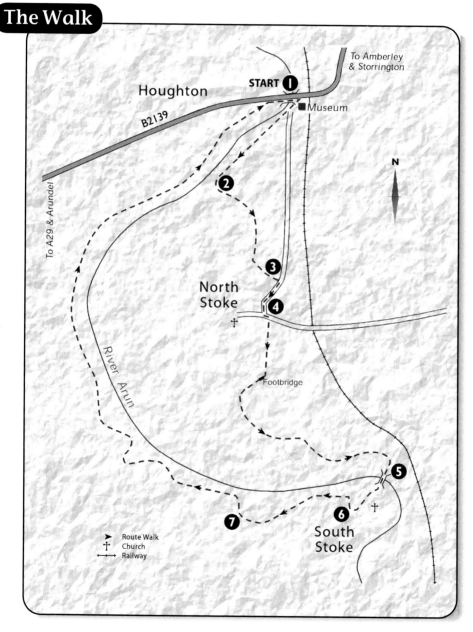

The River Arun below Houghton Bridge.

Refreshments You'll be spoilt for choice. The Amberley Working Museum has its own purpose-built, ultra modern Limeburners Restaurant (telephone: 01798 839240) serving snacks and light refreshments and the Bridge Inn (telephone: 01798 831619) offers daily specials. Over the road is the Houghton Bridge Riverside Tea Garden and Restaurant (telephone: 01798 831558).

Kiddiwalks in West Sussex

❶ Turn left along the road from the car parks of either of the first three refreshment options (turn right from the tea garden car park) and walk along the pavement to the bridge. Continue to the middle of the bridge. **Beware traffic. There is no pavement for 50 yards or so.** Go left over a stile, following a public footpath sign, and cross right over a second stile onto the riverbank. Cross a stile and continue for 80 yards to the bend in the river.

❷ Go left, following a sign over a stile, walking on a raised causeway to the lane.

❸ Turn right, weaving right and left uphill to the junction. *The hamlet of North Stoke is down the lane on the right.*

❹ Go left and immediately right and follow a public footpath sign,

◆ Background Notes ◆

In early times, the Arun was crossed by a ferry, **Houghton Bridge** being provided for the bishops on their way to and from Amberley. Twice during the 15th century, the bridge needed restoration, the bishop responsible for the second repairs encouraging the pledging of contributions by granting indulgences giving donors forty days respite from the pains of purgatory!

The **Toll House** at Houghton Bridge was built in 1813. The toll keeper received 8 shillings per week for his wage, fire and candles. The toll charge for coaches, landaus and chariots was 2 shillings.

North Stoke has a 13th century church in the care of the Churches Conservation Trust. Largely unaltered since the early 14th century, the building has a number of unique architectural features.

South Stoke was the home of Cyril Joad, teacher, philosopher, outcast and author who loved its peace and solitude; the rural idyll and his residency of South Stoke Farm inspired his last work of fiction *Folly Farm*. Its principal character – Mr Longpast – was self-based. The 11th century **St Leonard's church** occupies a halcyon spot near the river. Electricity only came to the hamlet in 1950 but the church is, unusually, still lit by candles. As you access the church, note the old carved initials on the quoin stones on the building to the right.

crossing two stiles and dropping down over a field to a boggy copse. Cross a stile and a suspension footbridge and walk on at the edge of woodland, crossing a stile left to the riverbank. Go left to the big farm bridge over the Arun.

5 Turn right over the bridge and swing right on a lane into South Stoke and pass St Leonard's church and cottages on the left. Swing right for 100 yards, passing the entrance to South Stoke Farm.

6 Turn right, following the bridleway sign at the back of the byre/barn that has obviously an ecclesiastical influence, and go left, following the sign, going right and left fieldside and dropping down to the fringe of a wood.

7 Go right at the bottom through a gate and swing left fieldside uphill. Drop down into woodland and follow the winding path. Swing right, passing the wall and the entrance to Arundel Park. Continue and merge with a broad track and, 100 yards before the next gate, go right (no sign) towards the river. Cross the planks over a ditch and cross a second planked ditch. Walk on to the bridge, crossing a stile and the bridge back to the starting point.